Letters from Hope Street:

A Collection of Lyrics and Poems

By Mark Anthony Mainardi

Registered member of ASCAP

Letters From Hope Street: A Collection of Lyrics and Poems

ISBN: 978-0-692-48388-6

Library of Congress

10 9 8 7 6 5 4 3 2 1

First Printing – August 2015

Proudly Printed in the United States of America

449 Productions
New Port Richey, FL 34653

All songs are registered with ASCAP
All photos are public domain and/or used with permission

For Stephanie,

"THIS is the story of our love!"

CONTENTS

A Word from the Author

This is an amalgamation of my work spanning over several decades…

These songs and poems range from: Young Love, to Heartbreak, to Marriage & Divorce, Divine Faith, Politics, Our Troops and the eternal journey of Self-Discovery. It is my hope that something in this book will resonate with your heart.

If you are a musician, writer or lover of music and would like to use or collaborate with me on any of my songs, please feel free to contact me at:

markanthonymainardi@gmail.com

Thank you and enjoy!
-Mark

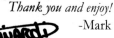

 Follow me on **Facebook:**
**Hope Street: A Collection of Lyrics and Poems
by Mark Anthony Mainardi**

 Mark Anthony Mainardi & 449 Productions are registered members with the American Society of Composers, Authors and Publishers

 ALL Proceeds from this book will be donated to the Wounded Warrior Project

All songs are under copyright and registered with ASCAP

SONGS

HOPE ST

AWAY FROM YOU

This is the breaking of my heart
I still don't understand
And I guess I never will
Love can be a bitter pill
When things don't work out
The way you planned

So shed a tear and I'll shed one too
We'll turn around and face the truth
I didn't mean to make you cry
It's always hard to say Goodbye
And I'll sit alone in this empty room
With my heart breaking into two
And find a way to make it through
As I move away from you

How did it ever come to this?
How could I never see
How you kept it all inside?
All those years you tried to hide
You were the one but not for me
So shed a tear and I'll shed one too
We'll turn around and face the truth
I didn't mean to make you cry
It's always hard to say Goodbye
And I'll sit alone in this empty room
Feel my heart breaking into two
And find a way to make it through
As I move away from you.

This is the breaking of my heart
I just hope that you're okay
And I know I was never there
But you know that I still I care?
As I slowly move away

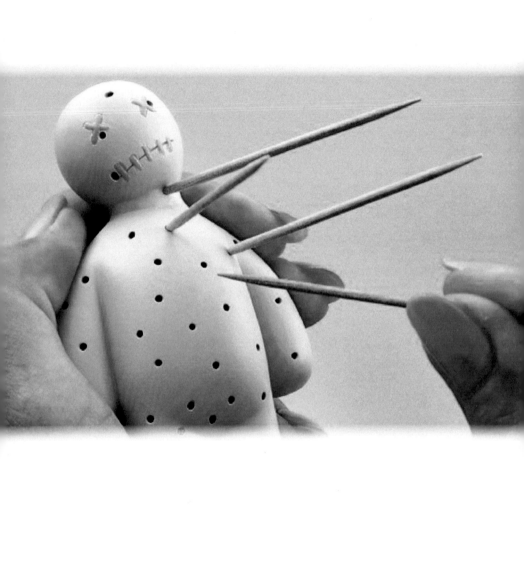

BETTER THAN OFF NOW

You, my dear, you walked away
With all your cryin' and your poutin'.
Been two days and a thousand nights
But then again who's countin'.
Time heals all wounds they say
But I think they got it wrong.
Sometimes it feels like yesterday
So today I wrote this song.

And Oh…
Skip. Dance. Run around
In my head I get no sleep
Last chance to bring me down
Enough's been said. Your talk is cheap
And Oh…
Are you better than off now?
Ah, Haa… Are ya better than off now?

I've been up, down, bounced around
In your pinball machine
You fooled me once and twisted twice
I think you know what I mean
But in spite of you I've changed so
much
So much, that I'm the same
There ain't no flies left on me
And baby you're to blame

And Oh…
Skip. Dance. Run around
In my head I get no sleep
Last chance to bring me down
Enough's been said. Your talk is cheap

And Oh…
Are you better than off now?
Ah, Haa… Are ya better than off now?
I laughed so much I lost control
Then the wheels went off the tracks
I wrecked the truck but saved my soul
Never gonna put up with your crap!

And Oh…
Skip. Dance. Run around
In my head I get no sleep
Last chance to bring me down
Enough's been said. Your talk is cheap
And Oh…
Are you better than off now?
Ah, Haa… Are ya better than off now?

And Oh…
Are you better than off now?
Ah, Haa… Are ya better than off now?
Better than off now
Better than off now
Better than off now!

BLONDIE BLUES and HENRY

Henry's on the roof again
"Man, I gotta change my scene."
Blondie-Blue cross-legged on the floor
Flippin' pictures in a magazine
Will she ever burn that bridge?
Will he ever make the time?
Will they ever find there's more to life
Than cheap champagne and wine?

Hey, Blondie! Blondie Blue Eyes
Is it hard to understand?
Hey, Blondie! Blondie Blue Eyes
You just do the best you can
What are you gonna do when the music
stops
And it's time to find a chair?
What are you gonna do when you come
home
And find that he's not there?
Poor Blondie, Blondie Blue Eyes
As you're rolling off in space
Poor Blondie, Blondie Blue Eyes
As the tears roll down your face

Don't ever let them tell you lies
Don't let them fade those blonde blue
eyes

Henry's on the streets again
"Boys, ain't this the life!"
Blondie-Blue picking out the rings
Will she ever be his wife?
Will she ever cross that threshold?
Will he ever settle down?
Will they ever find the strength, break
away
From their restless little town?

Hey, Blondie! Blondie Blue Eyes
Is it what the Bible said?
Hey, Blondie! Blondie Blue Eyes
Did your mama save your bed?
What are you gonna do when he stops
giving
All those diamonds and those pearls?
What are you gonna do when he starts
hanging
With those West-end little girls?
Poor Blondie, Blondie Blue Eyes
As you wish upon a star
Poor Blondie, Blondie Blue Eyes
How'd you let it get this far?

Don't run around with the wild guys
Don't let them fade those blonde blue
eyes

Hey, Blondie! Blondie Blue Eyes
Is it hard to understand?
Hey, Blondie! Blondie Blue Eyes
You just do the best you can
Don't ever let them tell you lies
Don't let them fade those blonde blue
eyes

BREAK YOU DOWN

I'm gonna break you down
Gonna turn you hard and cold
Whittle you down
Turn your heart into stone
One trip, one too many
Brought me down unto my knees
When I found your love
I wound up losing me

I'll tell you how it's done
How to sink this ship
Ya lay the ice and poke the hole
Light the match and watch it sink
You won't see this dog run circles
'round
Cuz when water lifts and love pulls you
down
I'm gonna break you down

I'm gonna break you down
Had all that I can take
Already had this love
Already made the same mistake
Been the master and the toy
Played the game of cat and mouse
Fell into a dream
Woke up to an empty house

I'll tell you how it's done
How to sink this ship
Ya lay the ice and poke the hole
Light the match and watch it sink
You won't see this dog run circles
'round
Cuz when water lifts and love pulls you
down
I'm gonna break you down

I'm gonna grab the wheel
And take back my control
Gonna reel you in
And hollow out your soul

I'll tell you how it's done
How to sink this ship
Ya lay the ice and poke the hole
Light the match and watch it sink
You won't see this dog run circles
'round
Cuz when water lifts and love pulls you
down
I'm gonna break you down

Cuz when your love bleeds
I'll leave no trace to be found
I'm gonna break you down

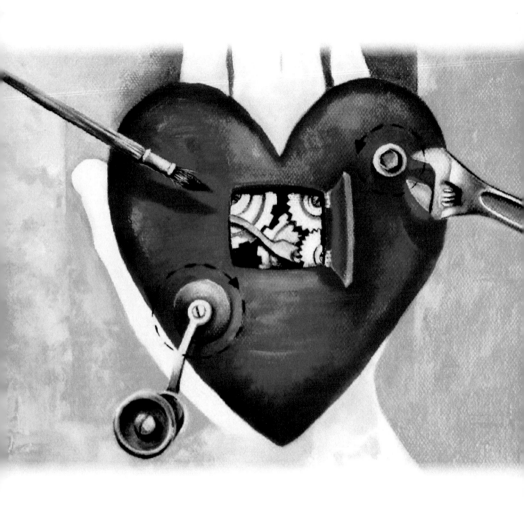

BUILDING MEMORIES

It only works if you let it
So, don't call it love and just forget it

So many men before me
Have written words of love by
candlelight
I'm no poet, it's plain to see
But I hope this time I got it right

Before I met you, life was spinning
Lost and out of control
But now you're here
Do you feel the same?
Or has this moment gotten old?
It only works if you let it
So, don't call it love and just forget it

Pushing, Pulling
Measure and trace
The gears are shiftin'
Wipe the sweat off of your face
Hear the assembly lines sing in reverie
We're building memories
We're building memories

Running to all the places
That others never dared to
Filling all the empty spaces
That no one really cared to
With all the words I left behind me
Written on a blank page
And still you find me
It only works if you let it
So, don't call it love and just forget it

Pushing, Pulling
Scream and shout
We're punchin' in and punchin' out
Shiny and new, riding out the factories
We're building memories
We're building memories

Pushing, Pulling
Hammer and nail
Shove and shoveling dreams into a pail
Blasting the smoke out of the chimneys
We're building memories
We're building memories

It only works if you let it
So don't call it love and just forget it

CAUGHT UP IN YOU

Big blue eyes and hot red lips
Telling me lies
With those long leather hips
I heard them call it "Sin"
I heard them call it "Sin"

Little Lolita stride
Coming down from the sky
With white velvet skin
Tell me, where to begin?
Tell me, where to begin?

Words won't change what time can't
heal
Even at the cost, this pain is too real
I've lost the moment and now she's
gone
Caught up in you…
Like a Taylor Swift song

She plays it tough, I play it cool
There are just some things
They don't teach you in school
And she won't let me in
And she won't let me in

Time will change what she can't feel
Experience is something that you can't
steal
It wears you down. She's not that strong
Caught up in you…
Like a Taylor Swift song

If she could only have seen her way
past him
We might have known what could have
been

Time will change what she can't feel
Experience is something that you can't
steal
It wears you down. She's not that strong
Caught up in you…
Like a Taylor Swift song
Windows throw shadows and I'm alone
Inside another bed, I'll call my home
These words and rhymes won't touch
her heart
Still caught up in you…
Like a Taylor Swift song

DAMAGED GOODS

I know it's hard to understand
To shine a light on who I am
Behind my eyes, you're looking for the
truth
In the back of a cab or in a booth
And your questions, they don't resonate
So, excuse me if I hesitate
I'm still blinded by my long forgotten
youth

Just a hopeless romantic with a heart
made of stone
Will paint you a picture of why I'm still
alone

I'm damaged goods. Left out in the rain
Dust piling up, rusting through my
brain
Still damaged goods and I'm not gonna
change
Cuz when you look behind my eyes
Damaged goods is what remains

There are some things I won't talk
about
Mysteries you can't figure out
You won't find my heart out on my
sleeve
Lies I told myself, I still believe
So, if you chose to stick around
Take all my little ups and downs
I won't be there to blame
If you decide to leave

I'm damaged goods. Left out in the rain
Dust piling up, rusting through my
brain

Still damaged goods and I'm not gonna
change
Cuz when you look behind my eyes
Damaged goods is what remains

There are compromises I've had to
make
Smiles wide I've had to fake
Still doing what I can to just survive
Some tears left inside I can revive
So don't judge me with that little frown
Cuz I'm not the only face around
There's a lot more like me
Left to be found

I'm damaged goods. Left out in the rain
Dust piling up, rusting through my
brain
Still damaged goods and I'm not gonna
change
Cuz when you look behind my eyes
Damaged goods is what remains
Just look behind my eyes
Damaged goods is what you'll find
I ain't ever gonna change
So, don't ask me to explain
I'm damaged goods, damaged goods
It's all the same
Damaged goods, damaged goods
Left in the rain

THE DREAM OF CORTEZ

Oh how far these eyes have seen
Long days of sailing blue and green
Windswept nights and purple seas
Swelled a vision that once sang to me
Oh how far these eyes have seen

My Soul has traveled tall
Upon the sea
Ever near my love to be
This weathered heart has journeyed
wide
To the edge of Heaven
Against her tide
To the edge of Heaven against her tide

Set out to sail in younger days
My book of life with moonlit gaze
Through seas of time I've sailed this
ship
Upon rolling tides and surly slips
Every list and yaw was meant to be
Oh how long these eyes have seen

My Soul has traveled tall
Upon the sea
Ever near my love to be
This weathered heart has journeyed
wide
To the edge of Heaven
Against her tide
To the edge of Heaven against her tide

Oh how low these eyes have turned
Away from God whose storm has
spurned
Of senseless rage and restless bliss
In squalls of fire I have burned
Oh how low these eyes have turned

My Soul has traveled tall
Upon the sea
Ever near my love to be
This weathered heart has journeyed
wide
To the edge of Heaven
Against her tide
To the edge of Heaven against her tide

Desperate, tied against the mast
A siren's song, her spell was cast
Hypnotic words retold to bend me
I pray, Oh Lord this day defend me

And now my quest has reached its end
This wicked Earth did twistly bend
Her footprints lay along the sand
I burn my ships at her command
So fallen deep, so deep, in song
Oh my love I've traveled long
Oh my love I've traveled long

EVERY DAY IS CHRISTMAS

Come and take a look up at the sky
It's Christmas morning in July
Sunshine kisses. Mistletoe
Snow on the beach
Come on let's go!

Every day is Christmas
Every day when I'm with you
Even though the sun is shining
The snow is falling down in June
Snowflakes all around us
Who would believe it but it's true
That every day is just like Christmas
Every day I spend with you

The summer sun can pack and run
He's in our way, His job is done
Pull out the carols, sing the songs
They'll call us crazy
But they're wrong

Every day is Christmas
Every day when I'm with you
Even though the sun is shining
The snow is falling down in June
Snowflakes all around us
Who would believe it but it's true
That every day is just like Christmas
Every day I spend with you

Fireflies in summer nights
Are glowing like those Christmas lights
It's what we feel and what we show
The sand is turning into snow

Every day is Christmas
Every day when I'm with you
Even though the sun is shining bright
The snow is falling down in June
Snowflakes all around us
Who would believe it but it's true
That every day is just like Christmas
Every day I spend with you
Every day is Christmas time
Every minute, every hour
It's enough to last all year
Love lingers long and has the power
Every day is like an ornament
That we hang when we are through
Cuz every day is just like Christmas
Every day I spend with you

FIRST KISS DRESS

It was just a matter of time before you
snuck behind
His back and stepped out. Now he
knows what you're about
He's a decent man and he won't
understand
Why you did him wrong. Pack up his
bags be gone

You'll have to win him back and you've
got the knack
To win his heart again. Maybe start
back as friends
Just give a little tear. Put on a little pout
I'm sure you've got this all figured out

Just make sure there's nothing you've
missed
Stick to the plan and check your list

Get that make-up just the way he likes
Tie up that hair all nice and tight
Push up that bra. Slide on them boots
Do all those things you used to do
And don't forget before you confess
To put on them tears
And that first kiss dress

You're putting Meryl Streep to shame
Honey, it's all part of your game
Why should it matter?
They all look still the same

Get that make-up just the way he likes
Tie up that hair all nice and tight
Push up that bra. Slide on them boots
Do all those things you used to do
And don't forget before you confess
To put on them tears
And that first kiss dress
This ain't your first Rodeo
It's time for another show
Until the next, first kiss dress

HEAR ME OUT

I know you've heard this all before
We've talked it out and talked it through
It's all been said, I'll say no more
There's only one thing left to do

We both been through some hard times
Hard times seem to come and go
But can't we go outside the lines?
Take a break from what we know?

Hear me out
Before you turn away
Hear me out
This doesn't have to take all day
Why does it have to be a fight?
I'm only asking for tonight
So before you scream and shout
Hear me out

If you look inside, you'll know it's true
It's something we both want to do
It isn't always black or white
Just say the word, I'll come tonight

Hear me out
Don't drag this on?
Hear me out
It don't take too long
To touch someone
Who makes you shake
It's not a crime or a mistake
It doesn't have to be forever
I only wanna be together
So before you scream
And before you shout
Hear me out

THE HUMAN HEART

Something in your eyes has changed
Something in your kiss is not the same
I won't be the one to let you pull away
No, I won't let you pull away

With love, there's no letting go
So before you run
I want you to know

The human heart is hard to heal
But love is worth it when it's real
You don't have to be afraid
You don't have to hold it in
We can dream and have it all
Love's not a game that you can win

I've finally put the past behind me
There's no one left to blame
There's nothing wrong with wanting
more
We don't have to be ashamed

It takes some patience and some time
So just hold on
And you will find

The human heart is hard to heal
But love is worth it when it's real
You don't have to be afraid
You don't have to hold it in
We can dream and have it all
Love's not a game that you can win

I'm not perfect. I make mistakes
There are many things I still don't know
Just take my hand and have some faith
We're all just learning as we go

The human heart is hard to heal
But love is worth it when it's real
You don't have to be afraid
You don't have to hold it in
We can dream and have it all
Love's not a game that you can win

I DON'T WANT TO LOSE YOU

I can feel you pulling away
Even though you tell me nothing's
wrong
I see you holding it in
I know you're doing your best and
trying to be strong
I don't want to lose you now
No, I don't want to lose you now

I've been crazy, maybe asking too much
You see it in me. I know that you're not
blind
I'd rather keep it inside and shut you
out
Than tell you what's on my mind
I don't want to lose you now
No, I don't want to lose you now

I can love you better than this
Believe it!
There's a better place for us
Can't you see it?
I can change. Turn it all around
You can bet me
And I can make it all worthwhile
If you let me

Because it's not easy for a man like me
To admit that he's been wrong
I take it out on you
Turn it into a fight but you knew that
all along
I don't want to lose you now
No, I don't want to lose you now

I've hurt too many people too many
times
And made up too many lies

It's all I knew at the time
But deep down inside, I know I never
tried
But I don't want to lose you now
No, I don't want to lose you now

I can love you better than this
Believe it!
There's a better place for us
Can't you see it?
I can change Turn it all around
You can bet me.
And I can make it all worthwhile
If you let me

So, let's start right here and right now!
I know I can make it work
I'll show you how
Starting now!

Cuz, I can feel us slippin' away
Even though you tell me nothing's
wrong
We're both holding it in but if we let it
all out
We'll come back twice as strong

I know you understand
Sometimes with love
It ain't easy to find your way
I'm still making mistakes
I'm doing my best and trying every day
And I don't want to lose you now
No, No, No, No, No, No
No I don't want to lose you now
Lose you now
I don't want to lose you

IN FRONT OF ME

Look behind these eyes and see the
truth
That little boy that waits for you
The truth lives on when we are gone
A silent voice that lingers on
Heaven is not within the stars
It's deep inside of who we are
The inner faith that brings release
That special place we find our peace

They don't know me…

They may see but they won't see
through me
They may try but won't know why
Standing right next to me
You were the one,
The one that I cried to,
The one that I tried to
Reach out in front of me

Darkness falls, I hold the light
Enough to see your face in mine
I turn it down and say "Goodbye"
Shadows fade the light that dies

They may see but they won't see
through me
They may try but won't know why
Standing right next to me
You were the one,
The one that I cried to,
The one that I tried to
Reach out in front of me

This moment is my truth
This moment is for you
This moment is my truth
This moment is for you

IT WAS YOU!

Cleopatra had it all
And ruled upon the Nile
Jackie O', told them "No"
With a dash of class and with style
Antoinette met her fate,
When she told 'em to eat cake
But there was always one long lass
To lead the way

And it was you!
Baby, it was you
Doing all those little things that you do
It was you
Honey, it was you
Even long before the rest
Darling, you were still the best
It's amazing what this thing
Has brought me to
Baby, it was you!

Mona Lisa has her smile,
And I guess that that's okay
Greta Garbo showed them all
Hit the top and walked away
And Miss Monroe could fill a dress
But lemme tell ya whadda mess
Still there was always one cool cat
Before the rest

And it was you!
Baby, it was you
Doing all those little things that you do
It was you

Honey, it was you
Even long before the rest
Darling, you were still the best
It's amazing what this thing
Has brought me to
Baby, it was you
She's a debutant. She's a tramp
A little angel and a vamp
I'm surprised you never met her
On the town
A dry Martini with a twist
She'll knock ya down with just one fist
Even when she keeps it home
She gets around

She's a tiger, she's a cat
She's sentimental and all that
Just get her started
And hard to slow her down
She's a model, she's a mouse
She'll place her bets and take the house
She's everywhere and still
She's nowhere to be found

Cuz Baby, it was you
Doing all those little things that you do
It was you
Honey, it was you
Even long before the rest
Darling, you were still the best
It's amazing what this thing
Has brought me to
Baby, it was you!

JUDGMENTIA

The hungry wheel is spurning
Turning mirrors on the mass
And candidates accentuate
Limo fires we can't pass
There's a hanging in the courtyard
A desperate act of their contrition
Screaming sounds, pulsate the room
Reveal the shame of this addiction

In our Judgmentia, we stand and shine
Ever deaf tone, flesh tone monuments
Of all our pain and pride
In our Judgmentia, let it live to watch
it die
No recompense for consciousness
There's a chance we won't survive

Under the microscope lights, burning
All the skin left for their feast
And poison slips in eloquence
While the blood hounds are released

There's a hanging in the courtyard
A desperate act of their contrition
Screaming sounds, pulsate the room
Reveal the shame of this addiction
In our Judgmentia, we stand and shine
Ever deaf tone, flesh tone monuments
Of all our pain and pride

Looking down, outside my window
I can see their wicked dance
Priests are praying and children playing
Marching lock-step in a trance

In our Judgmentia, we stand and shine
Ever deaf tone, flesh tone monuments
Of all our pain and pride
In our Judgmentia, we learn to come
alive
Killing all the willing
As they're walking in the tide
In our Judgmentia, you keep what you
can find
Ever pulling at the flesh
Of all the best we try to hide

LETTERS FROM HOPE STREET*
(A World Away From Me)

There's a little a box, underneath my
bed
Letters I wrote on the day that you left
We all drove from church to get to your
flight
I promised myself you would be alright

Find your way back home
You've been away from us too long
What do I tell our children
If something happens while you're
gone?
I touch the smile on your face
Coming from the picture screen
It's like we're both inside this room
But you're a world away from me
I see you everywhere
And my heart skips a beat
Ribbons on the ground
Letters from Hope Street

You in your uniform, so handsome and
bright
Sometimes even heroes make a sacrifice
As your plane lifted off, you waved
"good-bye"
I promised myself not to break down
and cry

Find your way back home
You've been away from us too long
What do I tell our children
If something happens while you're
gone?
I see the smile on your face
As I touch the picture screen
It's like we're both inside this room
But you're a world away from me
I see you everywhere
And my heart skips a beat
Ribbons on the ground
Letters from Hope Street

I hold your picture in my arms
Before I go to sleep
The pain deep inside
That no one else can see
Lay it down beside me
Where you used to be
Tying ribbons of love
Around your letters to me
Yellow ribbons of love
Letters from Hope Street

*Dedicated to ALL who serve this Great Country

LONG SUMMER SWAY

Hot, Odessa Night
Ya got me curled up tight
Just staring at the wall
The kids, are tucked in bed
Gotcha in my head
And waiting for your call

This house, is not my home
But it's all I've known
Sometimes it feels so strange
And you, falling from the sky
You make me wonder why
You'd wanna heal this pain

But Baby, I'm lonely and need
somebody
To touch me again
And maybe tonight, I could get it right
And feel alive again
It's so hard to be away
In this long summer sway

Love, is it just a dream?
Like some forgotten scene
In someone else's play?
I don't know, how far to go
But I think you know
Just tell me what to say

And now, ya got me all messed up
I think I've given up
I'm opening up my door
Come up and come inside
Let's take away our pride
And leave it on the floor

Cuz Baby, I'm lonely and need
somebody
To touch me again
And maybe tonight, I could get it right
And feel alive again
I can't wait another day
In this long summer sway
So, don't let it get away
In this long summer sway

LOVE IS OPEN

Hey little "little"
Got ya caught up in the middle
Of a motion drag you down
Creeping 'round without a sound
Because tonight, because tonight

Hey "Tippy-toe" just let it go
They never knew you and you know
It's a band and wagon town
Don't you let them hang around
Because tonight, because tonight

So, sweep the floors and turn the signs,
Unlock the doors and pull the blinds
Because tonight it's right on time
Because tonight it's right on time

Love is open soon
It's in our sight tonight.
It's on the move
Fireflies fill up the air
Spin around us everywhere
Ignite a light enough for two
Tonight our love is open soon

So learn to fly, Butterfly
I thought I saw it in your eyes
You tried to keep it underground
Kept it in the lost and found
Because tonight, because tonight

Just take it slow, let it grow
You're older now and don't you know
It's a band and wagon town
So, don't you let them bring you down
Because tonight, because tonight

So sweep the floors and turn the signs
Unlock the doors and pull the blinds
Because tonight it's right on time
Because tonight it's right on time

Love is open soon!
It's in our sight tonight,
It's on the move
Fireflies fill up the air
Spin around us everywhere
Ignite a light enough for two
Tonight our love is open soon

So, sweep the floors and turn the signs
Unlock the doors and pull the blinds
Reach for more, don't fall behind
Just let it soar and you will find
It was always right, it was always right,
It was always right before your eyes

THE LOVE OF A WOMAN

When you're stuck at home and sick in
bed
Who will hold your hand and kiss your
head?
You know when all is done and said
The love of a woman
When you've traveled past the county
line
Can't find your map or spare a dime
What will pick you up and be on time?
The love of a woman

You know, I've been around the world
And seen enough to see
There ain't nothing in this life
That ever comes close to be
What the love of woman has done to
me

When the wind blows and keeps you
guessin'
If your leaky roof has learned its lesson
What will find a room to rest in?
The love of a woman

You know, I've been around the world
And seen enough to see
There ain't nothing in this life
That ever comes close to be
What the love of woman has done to
me

Been written down through the ages
Been fought over, locked in cages
Thrown on the silver screen and stages
The love of a woman

So if one day true love finds you
I'll be right there to remind you
It might hurt and it might blind you
The love of a woman
Can turn a grown man into a boy
And all your sorrows into joy
It's the one thing words cannot destroy,
The love of a woman

You know, I've been around the world
And seen enough to see
What the love of a woman has done to
me

THE LOVE OF MY LIFE

When you touched my hand
I knew that my life
Would never be the same again
And the moment we kissed
It was what I had missed

When you touched my heart
You opened up the door
Sent it like a spark
That's when I knew I was sure
"I'm not alone anymore."

The love of a life comes once in a life
Just one life is all we have to live
The love of my life, waiting all of my life
For this love to begin

Every day her smile
And the way I feel
Walking down the aisle
I can't believe this is real
Finally found what is real

The love of a life comes once in a life
Just one life is all we have to live
The love of my life, waiting all of my life
For this love to begin

The love of my life, she's the heart of my life
Just one love is all we have to give
The love of a life, waiting all of our lives
For this love to begin
The love of my life
The love of my life

MAID OF HONOR

Woke up to a lazy lakeside
Hazy afternoon
Thought that I might still be dreaming
You slipped on your morning dress
Through silhouettes of sun
Winking smile as you were leaving

Everything is different now
Still I'm still the same
Was it the darkness that led me to
What remains?

Crying waiting in the wings
My Maid of Honor longs to be
In the center from the side
Who knows what tomorrow brings
My Maid of Honor, Bride to Be
When our yesterdays collide

White dress in the closet
Hangs of tribute and of faith
One day soon his pain will pass
Playing out these fairy tales
To mirrors in her room
Locked up in a locket
With a clasp

Everything is different now
Is she still the same?
Gone are the blue box and afterglows
And the blame

Crying waiting in the wings
My Maid of Honor longs to be
In the center from the side
Who knows what tomorrow brings
My Maid of Honor, Bride to Be
When our yesterdays collide

Wedding marches, christening, the
union of our lives
Whispering, the tears of nuptial vows
And all the brides, she stood beside,
now celebrate as wives
Like the doves that fly above us now

Crying waiting in the wings
My Maid of Honor longs to be
In the center from the side
Who knows what tomorrow brings
My Maid of Honor, Bride to Be
When our yesterdays collide

Who knows what tomorrow brings
When our yesterdays collide?

MISTER POWER TRIPPER

Mister Power Tripper
Third time's a charm
Unassuming tiny trickster
Up your sleeve and past your arm
Believing is easy, "Light and Breezy"
Ain't that what you sold me?
"I want you but I don't need you."
Isn't that what you told me?

Another heart for you to fling
In the land of the blind, you would be
King
Eyes shut open but you can't see
Just turn around and set me free

It isn't hard, Give it a try
Left foot, Right foot, pack up your bags
And wave "Goodbye"
You can put it in a letter and send it on
its way
Or be a man and shake my hand
Then turn around and walk away

Mister Power Tripper
Hanging yourself out on a cross
Hand to God, it wasn't her
In your maze of lies, I'm lost

Another notch put in your belt
What's the number? Who can tell
One plus one and one and me
Just turn around and set me free

It isn't hard, Give it a try
Left foot, Right foot, pack up your bags
And wave "Goodbye"
You can put it in a letter and send it on
its way
Or be a man and shake my hand
Then turn around and walk away

So, tell me the truth, one last, first time
In your Little Black Book
Was I a star or just a line?
I hope you're happy
Yes, So happy now with her
Maybe one day we can meet
Did she ever find my slipper?

Another heart for you to fling
In the land of the blind, you would be
King
Eyes shut open but you can't see
Just turn around and set me free

It isn't hard, Give it a try
Left foot, Right foot, pack up your bags
And wave "Goodbye"
You can put it in a letter and send it on
its way
Or be a man and shake my hand
Then turn around and walk away
Turn around and walk away
When there's nothing left to say
Just turn around and walk away

THE MOUNTAINS OF HOLLYWOOD

Say Goodbye, my friend
This place was like a centerpiece
We all knew it had to end
We lost our sunshine on the beach

Close calls and midnight calls
Getting tied up in the cross wires
Wind falls and free falls
Spreading ash from the fires

Will you come to me
When I do the things, I shouldn't do?
And shelter me
When their intentions aren't very good?
And rescue me
From the mountains of Hollywood?

Caught in the dark
Running on a spotlight
There's a man at Echo Park
Selling grace to save the night

Layovers and stay-overs
Leave the baggage up to fate
Makeovers that break over
Time and tide from gate to gate

Will you come to me,
When I do the things, I shouldn't do?
And shelter me,
When their intentions aren't very good?
And rescue me
From the mountains of Hollywood?

Take a chance
You always killed me with your smile
Learn the dance
You never lost your sense of style
Change is still the same
But you're not what we're looking for
Underneath the bed of shame
Fate is knocking down the door

Will you hold my hand
When my mood ring has turned to
blue?
And will you bring the sand
Build me castles with an ocean view?
Will you come to me,
When I do the things, I shouldn't do?
And find the room to hide behind
The mountains of Hollywood?

THE MUSIC OF YOUR HEART

Every day it grows deeper from inside
Like a light in the dark, from a lonely candle
When did I give up and learn to hide?
When did my life get too hard to handle?

Maybe it's me who needs to be found
Lost out at sea, waiting for direction
"Who's calling out? Is someone there?"
Words on the breeze from your warm affection

Will you be the arms to shelter me?
Sail out on a boat to rescue me?
And rock me gently mending
To the music of your heart

Eternal youth, so tender is your touch
To heal a heart so unrequited
I never knew love could mean so much
To feel the flame once again ignited

Will you be the arms to shelter me?
Sail out on a boat to rescue me?
And rock me gently mending
To the music of your heart

(Musical Bridge)

Will you be the arms to shelter me?
Sail out on a boat to rescue me?
And rock me gently mending
To the music of your heart
Be my eyes when I go blind?
Lead me on the floor and not behind
And dance me never-ending
To the music of your heart

THE NEXT LOVER

Been left on the roadside
Turned around and lost
This shiny little diamond
Needs some polishing off
It's harder looking down the road
Than it is to turn around
But there's nothing left to hold you
back
There's no one left to hold you down

Take a breath and take my hand
Don't you know who I am?
Don't you know who I am?
I'm the one to turn those lies around
To make them all come true
I'm the next lover to fall for you

There's a little town in Georgia
And everything you left behind
Little pieces of your heart
What you lost ain't hard to find
Ya can't lose, what's yours already
So, "come on, now" I know you're
ready

Start the dance, I'll start the band
Don't you know who I am?
Don't you know who I am?
I've always been beside you
When you thought your life was
through
I'm the next lover to fall for you

Time is passing out of touch
Moving past us every day
Use your heart
You think too much
There's nothing left to say

So hold on tight and don't let go
Take my hand and take it slow
Let me be your "start again"
Pick any wish and make it true
Just look at me and you will see
The next lover to fall for you

OWE IT ALL TO YOU

Gave up on love, till you came along
Now there is music and you are the
song
Every day is the first time
Since the day I met you
Now, there's love in my life and I owe it
all to you

Don't care what they tell me
I don't care what the cost
Without you beside me
I'd rather be lost
The days I've spent searching
Are now finally through
There's love in my life
And I owe it all to you

It may not be diamonds
It may not be gold
A love like ours baby, could never be
sold
Whatever life brings us, we will see it
through
There's love in my life and I owe it all
to you

And I don't care what they tell you
I don't care what the cost
Without you beside me
I'd rather be lost
The days I've spent wishing
Have finally come true
There's love in my life
And I owe it all to you

Love doesn't come to us all
Some people never at all
You can look but still never find
But Baby hold on
Cuz it's only a matter of time

And I don't care what they told you
I don't care what the cost
Without you beside me, I'd rather be
lost
The dream I was wishing
Has finally come true
There's love in my life
I have love in my life
You're the love of my life
And I owe it all to you

To you baby...
I owe it all to you

PUSSYCAT MASQUERADE

Dead locked, she's looking my way
Temper temptation bite of the wild
fruit
"Upstairs." What's to say?
Checking off in her little red "black
book"

Her coming up pictures explain,
Restless child wants more than money
Take them, they all look the same
Flip dime a chance, he's calling her
honey
Oh Honey…

Rattle those rat trapping toys
A velvet box, more faces than Janus
Disposable telephone boys
Making her faking me, taking, more
heinous
Cherry bomb ego eyes
They know what you hide…

I threw myself on the blade
Naked and bound, a slave to the tricks
trade
Threw myself on the blade
I'm coming in…
This Pussycat Masquerade

Velvetblackpoison in vain
Tapping away, they sweat and they
swagger
"Relax it's part of the game."
Leading him on with more cloak than
with dagger
It's easy to hide, when the size doesn't
matter
Cherry bomb ego eyes,
They know what you hide…

I threw myself on the blade
Naked and bound, a slave to the tricks
trade
Threw myself on the blade
I'm coming in…
This Pussycat Masquerade

Scratching our bodies to flames
Burning tattoos cut out in lip stains
A red badge of courage and blame
All you impress can attest to her hip
games

Bleed your excuses to waste
"So long" as long as you keep it in
shadows
But I'm caught on the hook as I taste
The sensual heat from beneath in the
gallows

I shouldn't be left in this primitive
wonder
But the hint of perfume in her room
Smells like hunger
Cherry bomb ego eyes,
They know what you hide…

I threw myself on the blade
Naked and bound, a slave to the tricks
trade
Threw myself on the blade
I'm coming in…
This Pussycat Masquerade

I'm coming in…
This Pussycat Masquerade
The Pussycat Masquerade

RED ROSES FOREVER

So this is it...
This is how it's meant to be
You hold my heart and not my hand
And with a line drawn in the sand
There's nothing left of you and me

And that's fine and that's okay
I'll keep it in so you won't know
And I know it's late, you have to go
But there's something left for me to say

Wherever you go
Whoever you love
I hope he brings you roses
Red roses
I hope he treats you kind
I hope he spends the time
We never spent together
I hope he brings you roses
Red roses forever

So here I am now, moving on
From everything I know that's true
From everything I know that's you
In a blink of time, it's dead and gone
And I know you want to leave
I won't try to make you stay
But there's something you should know
Before you turn and walk away?

Wherever you go
Whoever you love
I hope he brings you roses
Red roses

I hope he treats you kind
I hope he spends the time
We never spent together
I hope he brings you roses
Red roses forever

And now, is hope my consolation?
I'm lost in isolation
My world is upside down
And now, if I could only turn back time
We could leave this all behind
How could I ever be so blind?

So, wherever you are
And wherever you go
Whoever you love
More than you loved me
I hope he brings you roses
Red roses
And I hope he treats you kind
And I hope he gives you time
The time we'll never have together
I hope he brings you roses
Red roses forever

SHORTER THAN A CROW FLIES

I've seen you walking 'round the square
Smile drawn on your face
You make them all just stop and stare
You look so outta place
It's a tender trap when things go wrong
And you wind up back at home
But you haven't been away that long
Them grass roots don't stop growin'

And you...
You said that you would all do us proud
It was all over town
You...
You stretched that country mile too far
You can't change who you are
Shorter than a crow flies

It seems that all that city pride
Was nothing but a haze
They found you out, they kicked you
out
Your tail between your legs
They saw right through that little twang
Pounded hayseed into dust
Left some rope for you to hang
That pipe dream turned to rust

And you...
You said that you would all do us proud
It was all over town
You...
You stretched that country mile too far
You can't change who you are
Shorter than a crow flies

We knew it was all in your mind
How could you leave us behind?
You burned that bridge back to town
Why are you hanging around?

And you...
You said that you would all do us proud
It was all over town
You...
You stretched that country mile too far
You can't change who you are
Shorter than a crow flies
Shorter than a crow flies
Backin' up your "Goodbyes"
Shorter than a crow flies

THE SIRENS OF AMOUR

For as long as,
For as long as I have journeyed
I have followed,
I have followed sirens singing
With the moon behind my back
And the stars above my eyes
Without compass, without map
I have rendered to the tides

And it's my wonder,
It's my wonder in this journey
That has cursed me,
That has cursed this quest damnation
Crossing oceans of time
To the lands of Babylon
Under Scandinavian skies
To the shores of Avalon

Far…
Beyond the Asian sea
Far…
Beyond all memory

Let their singing by the shore
Lead me to the ocean floor
Crash this ship against the moor
By the spell of their allure,
And search the Earth forevermore
For the Sirens of Amour

And this vision,
And this vision I've let haunt me
Kept me searching,
Kept me searching ever after… and
after
The ones who sang to me,
High upon Copernicus
To the storms of Galilee
A voyage through Aquarius

Far…
Beyond all destiny
Far…
To my insanity

Let their singing by the shore
Lead me to the ocean floor
Crash this ship against the moor
By the spell of their allure
Cross this barren heart once more
For the Sirens of Amour
Let their singing by the shore
Lead me to the ocean floor
Crash this ship against the moor
By the spell of their allure
To search the Earth forevermore
For the Sirens of Amour

SO FAR, SO GOOD!

I know you're watchin'
Yes, I know who you are
You think we're going too far
I see you watchin'
I hear you're guessin'
You think we're going too fast
I hope you're having a blast
You have our blessin'
Take a look inside yourself
And if you care to know,
Here's how we're doin'

So far, so good
It all worked out
The way that it should
So far, so good
You said we couldn't
And we knew that we could
So far and so good

You confirmed it
We knew it right from the start
You hadda hole in your heart
Because you've burned it
Just take a look inside yourself
And if you care
Here's how we're doin'

So far, so good
It all worked out
The way that it should
So far, so good
You said we couldn't
And we knew that we could
So far and so good

This wasn't planned out
But still it panned out
There ain't no big explanation
The wedding bells cheer
So, "go to Hell dear!"
This is our grand invitation

And if you need to know
Here's how we're doin'

So far, so good
It all worked out
The way that it should
So far, so good
You said we couldn't
And we knew that we could
So far and so good
We made it work
Like we said that we would
So far and so good
Sometimes love fits
The way that it should, so far
And so good!

THE STORY OF OUR LOVE

So when they ask us how we did it
We'll just look at them and say

The story of our love was written
With words from in our hearts
It's filled with picture pages
And never-ending where it starts
We'll take it down from off the shelf
To let it shine in all its glory
This is the life that we have lived
This is our love story

So many people live their life without
love
Why did we get so lucky? How did we
get so lucky?
So many lonely nights, living without
love
Without you near this way. Without you
here today

So when they ask us how we did it
We'll just look at them and say…

The story of our love was written
With words from in our hearts
It's filled with picture pages
And never-ending where it starts
We'll take it down from off the shelf
To let it shine in all its glory
This is the life that we have lived
This is our love story

So many hearts broken but only a few
are chosen
And we feel it and we're lucky. Every
single day we're lucky
So many rainbows rising and it's still so
surprising

That it swept us both away. We knew it
long before today

So when they ask us how we did it
We'll just look at them and say…

The story of our love was written
With words from in our hearts
It's filled with picture pages
And never-ending when it starts
We'll take it down from off the shelf
To let it shine in all its glory
This is the life that we have lived
This is our love story

One Day, One Kiss,
One Touch, One Moment
One Day, One Kiss,
One Touch, One Moment
This is our love story

So when they ask us how we kept it
going
This is what we'll say
That time and tide has kept love
growing
Long before today

The story of love was written
With floating bottles on the ocean
Like shooting stars across the sky
A timeless tale of hearts in motion
With every life that's left to live
With every love that's left to give
Told to the young and all before me
This is our love story

One Day, One Kiss
One Touch, One Moment

TENDER LIFE

It makes you scream and makes you cry
It doesn't mean you have to die
We all make the same mistakes
A little faith is all it takes
In this life

Now you're reaching out your hand
I know it's hard to make a stand
Just hold on tight with all your might
It won't take long to see the light
In this life

This Tender Life
Whoa Oh, Yeah
Ya gotta get it right
Whoa Oh, Yeah
And it don't come twice
Whoa Oh, Yeah
So just hold on tight
Whoa Oh, Yeah
To this Tender Life

You can't turn back the hands of time
So just take what you can find
And you can leave the past behind
It's in your heart and not your mind
In this life

All the roads that you have turned
And all the bridges that you've burned
Will help you find your way back home
You won't ever be alone
In this life

This Tender Life
Whoa Oh, Yeah
Ya gotta get it right
Whoa Oh, Yeah
It don't come twice
Whoa Oh, Yeah
So just hold on tight
Whoa Oh, Yeah
To this Tender Life

You can scream and you can cry
It doesn't mean you have to die
In this life

THANX FOR LETTING ME SHARE

Folks, lemme tell it to ya straight
Put it out there from the start
I'm hard-hearted one
With ice run through my heart
Cold as a dark December
Shine the light then turn to dust
Like a pounding rain
Let my love turn into rust

"So, what's the bottom line?
What's it all worth living for?"
I can feel your stares
You've probably heard this all before
I keep telling myself
"I'm not gonna change."
But then it starts again
What was I just thinking of?
This can't be love

I did my "one forever"
Danced me till the end of time
But then the song changed
Stopped forever on a dime
And the one score I could count on
Big bouncing beds against the wall
It would take all night
If I had to name them all

"So, what's the bottom line?
What's it all worth living for?"
I can feel your stares
You've probably heard this all before
I keep telling myself
"I'm not gonna change."
But then it starts again
What was I just thinking of?
This can't be love

I really wish you'd give me something
So I could make this stop
Is there something I could smoke?
Some pill that I could pop?
I really don't think it's funny
So, wipe that smile off your face
Don't you speak my language?
Have I come to the right place?

"Is she the bottom line?
The one I've been waiting for?"
It hurts when she's not there
I've never felt like this before
I put my hand on my chest
"I'm gonna have to change."
But did I start too late?
Am I the one she's thinking of?
Do you think this is love?

THAT'S MY LIFE

You may think I'm not that smart
Or you might think I hold the key
Either way I've played the part
Of every role you've had for me

You know it's true!
Hey, Would I lie to you?

Cuz that's my life and Baby, I love it!
They say, "Don't push your luck."
And I try to shove it
Can't grow wings or rise above it
That's my life and baby, I love it

Some may have figured me out
"He's just the sizzle not the steak."
But don't you ever count me out
That would be your last mistake

Now, I see you're turning blue
Well, I've got some things to do

Cuz that's my life and Baby, I love it!
They say, "Don't push your luck."
And I try to shove it
Can't grow wings or rise above it
Cuz that's my life and baby, I love it

I may not have your style
I may not have your class
But baby when you hear that bell
You can all just kiss my ass!

Cuz I always have a back-up plan
Just waiting for the kill
And when I finally cross that finish line,
I'll be singin' to ya still…

That that's my life and Baby, I love it!
They say, "Don't push your luck."
And I try to shove it
I can't grow wings or rise above it
Cuz that's my life and baby, I love it
It's my life and baby, I love it

TICK TOCK

It's a little "scary" scary
Lying next to you
Sometimes I dunno what to say
I get so nervous, don't what to do
Come and kiss me with your smile
Set your eyes in mine
Just take it slow and make it sweet
We've got the time

I sit alone in my room
Just a waitin' for you
Stare at the door and the clock
And I know I should stop
Crawlin' outta my skin
When will this night begin?
And my heart it goes tick tock
Tickity Tock.

I try to keep it all together
Still I'm so confused
I try to look away
You read my mind. I'm so in love with
you
You're lightning in a bottle
A little closer baby, dance with me
I think it's crazy how we got here
You're a mystery

I sit alone in my room
Just a waitin' for you
Stare at the door and the clock
And I know I should stop
Crawlin' outta my skin
When will this night begin?
And my heart it goes tick tock
Tickity Tock

Blow out the candles. Make a Birthday
wish
Shoot it like an arrow and you'll never
miss
Every day is Valentine's with you
I'll draw it in the sky and send it back
to you
I love you, Love you
Love love, love love, love you!!

I sit alone in my room
Just a waitin' for you
Stare at the door and the clock
And I know I should stop
Crawlin' outta my skin
When will this night begin?
And my heart it goes tick tock
Tickity Tock
Time is falling behind
I think I'm losing my mind
And my heart it goes tick tock
Tickity Tock

WHY YOU GOTTA BE MAKIN' ME?

I think I'm freaking out!
Did I just say that out loud?
Two ain't enough and three is a crowd
But I'm under your spell
Walking 'round in my sleep
I may be going insane
But the ticket is cheap

And I'm walking into ditches
Bumping into the walls
Falling off of bridges
My friends don't know me at all
I should pull myself together
But all I think about is you
So, why you gotta be makin' me
Fallin' for you?

I try to behave but I'm starting to stare
I can't even breathe
She's gonna know that I'm there

I roll over laughing
Dropping things on the floor
Can't even drive
I close my hands on the door
I know that I'm crazy
You're too good to be true
So, why you gotta be makin' me
Fallin' for you?

Head over heels
From my head to my toes
Riding this rocket
I don't care where it goes
I might be flying too high
But I'm enjoying the view
So, why you gotta be makin' me
Fallin' for you?

I shake and I sweat
Feeling weak in my knees
Put my hands on my heart
Can I have some more please?
I'm screaming out your name
Cuz I don't know what to do
So, why you gotta be makin' me
Fallin' for you?

YOU LOVE ME TOO

I can't find a place to start with you
Can't sail my broken heart to you
Or drop it from the clouds above
No matter how I try to reach for you
I can't find the words to speak to you
Or prove to you that this is love

So, I've thought it out and I've thought
it through
And this is what I'm gonna do…

I'm gonna stop the Earth dead in its
motion
Crash all the stars into the ocean
Whatever it takes to get to you
Rip the Sun out from the sky
Let all the rivers run dry
This is what I'm gonna do
Until I hear you love me too

I can't find another way to get to you
It doesn't matter what I say to you
It's still him you're thinking of
I can't cry enough tears to make you see
All the things you mean to me
There's just no way to rise above

But now, I've thought it out and I've
thought it through
And this is what I'm gonna do…

I'll take all the storm clouds from the
plains
And drown the deserts in the rain
No matter what it takes, to see this
through
Run all the clocks out of their time
And lay my life down on the line
This is what I'm gonna do
Until I hear you love me too

No matter how I try to reach for you
I can't find the words to speak to you
So I've thought it out and I've thought
it through
And this is what I have to do…

But be the voice inside your head
Creeping up inside your bed
Sending chills throughout your spine
The night won't hide you in your room
I'll set fire to the moon
And never stop until you're mine
This is what I'm gonna do
Until I hear… You love me too

YOU'RE A GIFT TO ME

There's one less letter in Santa's box this
year
I'm sure he has enough to do
With every child whispering in his ear
Of secret wishes, dreams come true
There's one more stocking by the
fireplace
With one new name upon its sleeve
Another picture, smiling faces
To lighten up this Christmas Eve

I don't need to make a list this year
Of gold and silver in a shop
Why take the time to write it down?
When there's only one word at the top

You're the only gift I want for
Christmas
You're a gift to me
There's nothing else I'd rather have
Underneath my tree
So if they ask me what I want this year
It should be easy for them to see
You're the only gift I want for
Christmas
You're a gift to me!

If you took all the gold in Fort Knox
And every diamond sold at Tiffany's
Put 'em all inside a great big box
With a card addressed to me
It wouldn't be worth a single dime
Or the box and bow you set
It would never equal all the time
We've spent together
Since the day we met

I don't need to make a list this year
Of gold and silver in a shop
Why take the time to write it down?
When there's only one word at the top

You're the only gift I want for
Christmas
You're a gift to me
There's nothing else I'd rather have
Underneath my tree
So if they ask me what I want this year,
It should be easy for them to see
You're the only gift I want for
Christmas
You're a gift to me

You're the gift that keeps on giving
Let's settle down and make a living
And when the children have come and
gone
We'll snuggle up and sing this song

You're the only gift I want for
Christmas
You're a gift to me
There's nothing else I'd rather have
Underneath my tree
You can't put a price on the things that
matter
Some of the best things in life are free
You're the only gift I want for
Christmas
You're a gift to me!

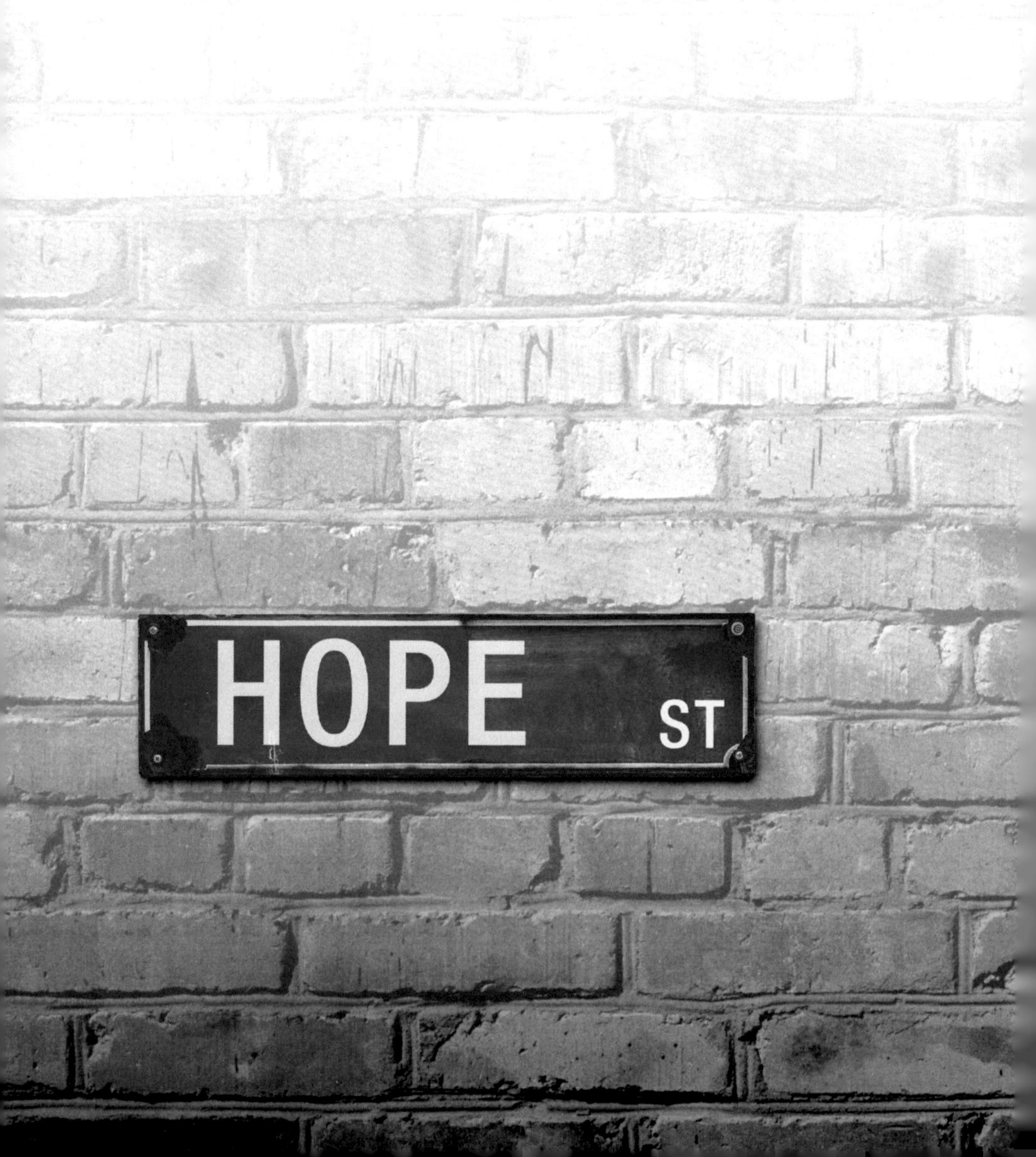
HOPE ST

POEMS

A PRAYER FOR HUMILITY

LORD,
Allow me to see the happiness
That grows inside my soul
To celebrate my life by living
For the measure of who I am
Rests in You alone

And fear is an illusion
True joy is a heart at rest
With You by my side
Right now and forever
With Your guidance, I am blessed

LORD,
Let me live within this world
You have created,
Walking by faith and not my sight
Ever patiently I've waited
Carry me in Your loving light

And when I lay my soul
Down to repent
I will meet You at the gate
And give You back this life You lent
as we vanish in YOUR grace

BELONGING

Are you really there?
When it gets too much to bear
Can you hear my hopes and prayers?
And when I'm hurting
Do you care?

Is there something left to prove?
Some other path that I should choose?
Any mountains I can move?
That's why I'm on my knees, now
Asking you…

Do you belong to me or to them?
Are you the voice inside my head?
Tell me, what happens when we're
dead?
Do you belong to me or to them?

Trying to please is an endless task
When a leap of faith is all you ask
But will you catch me if I crash?
Please catch me if I crash

That's why I'm on my knees, now
Asking you…

Do you belong to me or to them?
Are you the voice inside my head?
Tell me what happens when we're dead?
Do you belong to me or to them?

Are you real or just a dream?
Sometimes it gets so hard to see
What to hold and to set free?
Is it them or is it me?

So, are you really there
When it gets too much to bear?
Do you hear my hopes and prayers?
And when I'm hurting
Do you care?

Tell me…
Are you really there?

DRIVE YOU AWAY

In the summer sun, we were so young
Just having fun, we took a fall
Not much around to be found
We'd leave this town. We'd show them
all
Packed all the bags and honked the
horns
We said our peace. We stood so tall

I will drive you away
From the world you've always known
I'll turn my heart into your home
I will drive you away
Look straight ahead and leave your
sorrows
We'll fill today with love's tomorrows

We started out and started strong
We lingered long and chased our pride
Tried to grow but grew apart
The grass grew greener on one side

Closing doors and silent floors
Hear only echoes of a dance
You drift apart. You let it go
You keep the love but lose romance

Will I drive you away?
From the love you've always known?
There's nothing left to make a home
Will I drive you away?
Looking out on empty spaces
Pictures fade but not the faces

Call it by another name
Did we look at love the same?
They say it takes a little time
But that was what we couldn't find

Did I drive you away?
From the youth set in your eyes
From golden days of summer skies
Did I drive you away?
Reaching out inside the dark
There's nothing left to hold my heart

DRIVEWAY DAYS

We were pirates in the night
On wayward trips into the sun
Sailing high on floating ships
A band of misfits on the run

Living life, when life was new
It was all we ever knew

In driveway days, we never grew old.
Time was short. Tall tales were told.
Looking back, as pictures fade
Their colors run to driveway days.

We were searching for ourselves
To find the "meaning of it all"
And when we couldn't find the answers
We made them up and went along

Living life, when life was new
It was all we ever knew…

In driveway days, we never grew old.
Time was short. Tall tales were told.
Looking back, as pictures fade
Their colors run to driveway days.

They were the best of times that you
regret
But what you left behind, I won't forget
The highs and lows and games we
played
It took your heart but mine remained

Those driveway days are hard to fill
When friends were friends
And time stood still
Sometimes it feels like yesterday
That brings me back to driveway days

It was all we ever knew

FROM MY TELLTALE HEART

…And if you should forget
Speak these words as a prayer
From my telltale heart

I want you more and more again
From beginning to the end
Nothing wasted, ever wanting
I want you more and more again

And should you forget
Sing it like a song unto your heart
Of rainbows rising, sunsets sleeping
Let it melt you from the start

I want you time and time once more
For every word set down to page
For every moment that we touch
I want you time and time with age

And should you forget
Forget me not, nor lover's end
In rooms of roses, rain-soaked letters
That time and tide forgot to send

And if I should forget
Pick me up just like a feather
And whisper wishes, wishes true
When these wishes were once new
Pick me up again, my lover
Pick me up again, for you

HEARTS FALLEN SHATTERED

If I could have one night's sleep
Or even have one tear to keep
Maybe we could start over again
Maybe find some room to bend

It doesn't have to be this hard
It doesn't have to be this mean
There's no point in us yelling
We don't have to make a scene
We always knew this day would come
Now two is broken into one
Hearts fallen shattered and I'm scarred
It doesn't have to be this hard

If you could ever try to let it go
Take off the mask I've come to know
And finally show me who you are
Then the distance that's between us
Wouldn't have to be this far

It doesn't have to be this hard
It doesn't have to be this mean
There's no point in us yelling
We don't have to make a scene
We always knew this day would come
Now, two is broken into one
Hearts fallen shattered and I'm scarred
It doesn't have to be this hard

Woke up to a face I couldn't recognize
Was it all just a part of her disguise?

It didn't have to be this hard
We could have turned and walked away
There's only pain and empty silence
When there's nothing left to say
We always knew this day would come
A million tomorrows minus one
Hearts fallen shattered and I'm scarred
It doesn't have to be this hard
I gave an inch, you took a yard
It didn't have to be this hard

I WILL SURRENDER

There's a spy in the house of love
There's a storm that's raging from
above
I can feel it coming, I can feel it coming
In a midnight message sent to me
Your whispered wish of ecstasy
And I can feel you coming
And I can feel you coming

Desperate fingers fondle fantasy
Ignite the fire deep inside of me
I can feel it coming, I can feel it coming
Pounding Passion's Hungry Hearts
A Lover's Promise Ripped Apart
And I can feel you coming
And I can feel you coming

There's an aching underneath my skin
There's a heat that's bursting from
within
Behind my body, pulling back
Lost and caged inside your trap
I touch the flame and ride the deep
It cuts so hard, I'm yours to keep
With every touch, I still remember
Caught in your arms, I will surrender

And in this madness, I am free
Leaving everything I know
Taking all the sadness left in me
I cannot hide it anymore
No more masks and no more scars
I hear the lightning hit the ground
You shelter me within your arms
Then suddenly there is no sound

A hunter sets to track me down
My body shakes and spins around
I feel you coming, I feel you coming
Hidden down paths of mystery
Reckless burns intensity
And I feel you coming
And I feel you coming

Helpless, Drowning, Hard to breathe
Gasping for the air, you're all I need
I reach for you, No turning back
From desperate eyes of your attack
I touch the flame and ride the deep
It cuts so hard, I'm yours to keep
This lasting lust I will remember
Caught in your arms...
I will surrender

THE MUSIC OF YOUR HEART

Every day it grows deeper from inside
Like a light in the dark, from a lonely candle
When did I give up and learn to hide?
When did my life get too hard to handle?

Maybe it's me who needs to be found
Lost out at sea, waiting for direction
"Who's calling out? Is someone there?"
Words on the breeze from your warm affection

Will you be the arms to shelter me?
Sail out on a boat to rescue me?
And rock me gently mending
To the music of your heart

Eternal youth, so tender is your touch
To heal a heart that's been unrequited
I never knew love could mean so much
To feel the flame once again ignited

Will you be the arms to shelter me?
Sail out on a boat to rescue me?
And rock me gently mending
To the music of your heart

Will you be the arms to shelter me?
Sail out on a boat to rescue me?
And rock me gently mending
To the music of your heart
Be my eyes when I go blind?
Lead me on the floor and not behind
And dance me never-ending
To the music of your heart

NEVER ALONE

I met this guy at a coffee shop
His hands were shaking. Beaten down
Said he couldn't stop
Couldn't keep his eyes from off the
clock

I used to be that man, not long ago
Hidden voices whisper but never show
Death can creep so very slow

But now the mask is gone
The lie is dead
There's only one voice in my head
And that voice is me
I'm powerless, I'm free!

My conscience slept in vain,
Living lies that I believed
There must have been an angel
That was watching over me
Because I never heard the sound
Of my mother as she wept
A higher power lifting, guiding
Brought me to my home
And whispered in my ear
That I'm never alone

I didn't need those back rooms
anymore
So I tore this house down to its core
Let the broken glass lay on the floor

But the thought that seemed to cross
my mind
That in those shattered dreams, I left
behind
Were all the missing pieces I could
never find

I'm human now. Not insane
A resurrection beyond name
Only to find me, surrendering
To be

I was full of shame,
Brought down to my knees
There must have been an angel
That was watching over me,
Cuz I never hit the ground
From the building when I leaped
A higher power lifting, guiding
Brought me to my home
And whispered in my ear
That I'm never alone

I met this guy at a coffee shop
His hands were shaking. Beaten down
Said he couldn't stop
Couldn't keep his eyes from off the
clock

STEPPING INTO THE LIGHT

For so long I thought I walked alone
Never knowing you were by my side
Couldn't find a place to call my home
Thought it was enough to just survive

But then the darkness
Brought me to my knees
That's where I found the faith
You had in me

Stepping into the light
You were always there beside me
Your loving voice to guide me
It's time I gave up on the fight
And let this spirit take to flight
Stepping into the light
Stepping into the light

Every day He's with me everywhere
I can see Him in my child's face
I can hear Him calling out to me
I can feel His love and tender grace

And all these blessings
Bring me to my knees
I'm grateful for each day
You've given me

Stepping into the light
You were always there beside me
Your loving voice to guide me
To "Just let go" without a fight
And let my spirit take to flight
Stepping into the light
Even though the road is long
He gives me strength to carry on
And now I see it burning bright
I'm stepping into the light

ACKNOWLEDGEMENTS

This book would not have been possible without the inspiration, support, comments, cheerleading and incredible photos from the love of my life: Stephanie Nicole Dye, who shows me every day, what it means to love and to be loved. My heart and life are enriched to have her in it...today and for years to come. "I love you Berby."

To Bob Jordan: my friend, my sounding board and my compass. His love and guidance is something that could never be repaid or replaced. Bob has given me the presence of a father, where there once was none. "Thank you and I love you Frasier."

To my lovely editor Pamela Sapio, for showing me that: "three dots... are better than four!"

My deepest thanks to: David Foster, Diane Warren, Walter Afanasieff, James Horner (may he rest in the same peace that his music gave us), Kenneth Brian Edmonds, Sir Paul, John, George & Ringo, Billy Martin Joel, Sara Bareilles, Elton John & Bernie Taupin, Kenny Loggins, Don Henley, Simon, Nick, John, Roger & Andy, Barry & Neil, Francis Albert Sinatra, Phil, Mike & Tony, Gordon Sumner, Taylor, Isaac and Zac, Martie, Emily & Natalie, Andrea, Caroline, Sharon & Jim, and to Frank & Lori, for exposing me to some of these artists when I was tall enough to put the needle on the vinyl.

And finally, to anyone and everyone who has ever walked into a room and asked for help. If I can do it, you can do it... "So go out and do it, because there will never be another NOW!"